J 95
Stee   W9-BBM-218
Afghanistan : from war to
peace?

$29.25
ocn779873656
1st ed.   01/15/2013

Afghanistan
from War to Peace?

Afghanistan
from War to Peace?

Philip Steele

rosen publishing's
rosen central

New York

Published in 2013 by The Rosen Publishing Group, Inc.
29 East 21st Street, New York, NY 10010

First Edition

Library of Congress Cataloging-in-Publication Data

Steele, Philip, 1948–
Afghanistan: from war to peace?/Philip Steele.—1st ed.
    p. cm.—(Our world divided)
Includes bibliographical references and index.
ISBN 978-1-4488-6030-2 (library binding)
1. Afghanistan—Juvenile literature. 2. Afghanistan—History, Military—Juvenile literature. 3. Afghanistan—Foreign relations—Juvenile literature. I. Title.
DS351.5.S77 2012
958.1—dc23

2012010616

Manufactured in the United States of America

CPSIA Compliance Information: Batch #S12YA: For further information, contact Rosen Publishing, New York, New York, at 1-800-237-9932.

Contents

Chapter 1
The long war

Helmand province is a dry and dusty region, baked by the sun in summer. It lies in the flat scrublands of southern Afghanistan. In recent years Helmand has seen bitter fighting. Soldiers have been shot and roadside bombs have blown up army vehicles.

In 2010 an army camp at Nahr-e-Saraj, known as Patrol Base 3, was at the center of this storm. It was occupied at the time by British troops, Ghurkha soldiers from Nepal and Afghan government forces. Their enemies were insurgents, known generally as the Taliban.

On the night of July 13, 2010, an Afghan soldier who was on guard at the base, Sergeant Talib Hussein, shot dead a British officer, Major James Joshua Bowman, as he slept in his tent. He then fired a rocket-propelled grenade into the Company Operations Room, killing Lieutenant Neal Turkington and Corporal Arjun Purja Pun. In the confusion, Hussein fled.

Some days later a man claiming to be Hussein contacted news networks, saying that he was now being sheltered by the Taliban, and that he had carried out the killings because the British troops were "killing innocent people."

Had Hussein been a Taliban agent all along? If so, that was strange – for the sergeant belonged to the Hazara ethnic group, who had themselves been targeted by the Taliban. Most Taliban fighters come from another ethnic group, the Pashtun. Did Hussein have connections with other militant groups? Or was he acting on his own? Many questions still remain unanswered.

The Western press was also asking bigger questions. Were the Afghan government forces reliable allies? Was this war being fought in the right way? Was it a just war? Whose interests was it serving? Could it be won? When might it end? Those questions, too, remain unanswered.

The tragic deaths of these soldiers devastated their families and friends. Many other families had endured similar grief. By February 2011, 2,318 foreign soldiers had been killed in Afghanistan. Of these, 1,472 were Americans, 352 were British and 494 were from other allied armies. Thousands of insurgents had been killed. Many thousands of Afghan civilians had also been killed by both sides, from bombing, terrorist acts and a breakdown of law and order. In 2010 alone, 2,777 Afghan civilians were killed and more than 3,720 were injured, according to the United Nations.

Afghanistan has seen war for many years. This latest conflict is one phase in a very long history. On the one side is a multi-national force, with the greatest number of troops coming from the United States and the United Kingdom, fighting alongside the Afghan national army. There are also currently about 40,000 privately contracted armed security guards working in Afghanistan. On the other side are supporters of the Taliban, an alliance of Muslim militias and political factions, which formed the government in Afghanistan from 1996 to 2001. The Taliban aimed to clear up the lawlessness, chaos and corruption, which had resulted from years of war. However, their violent punishments and suppression of opponents soon made them many enemies, at home and abroad. Today the Taliban have been joined by individuals from other countries who believe they are fighting in defense of Islam, and by nationalists who simply oppose the presence of foreign troops. Some insurgents are fighting for money, land or power. The conflict has also spilled across the border into neighboring Pakistan.

This book looks at how and why this long war has happened. It considers the aims of both sides and how it might be ended. It discusses government, religion and human rights, economics and international aid. And it asks, can a lasting peace be built in the future?

▲ *In Helmand in 2010, an Afghan boy watches anti-Taliban soldiers go on patrol. The troops are Gurkhas of the British army and Afghans from the government forces.*

Chapter 2

From past to present

When the leaders of the West went to war in Afghanistan in 2001, had they read their history books? This question was asked at the time because of the failure of past military actions in the region. Irregular Afghan fighters had taken on the British Empire at the height of its power, between 1839 and 1919, and inflicted a major defeat in 1842. From 1979 another of the world's most powerful armies, that of the Soviet Union (now the Russian Federation), battled for ten years with Afghan resistance fighters before withdrawing from the country. Could a foreign army ever really win a war against local guerrillas in the remote, mountainous terrain?

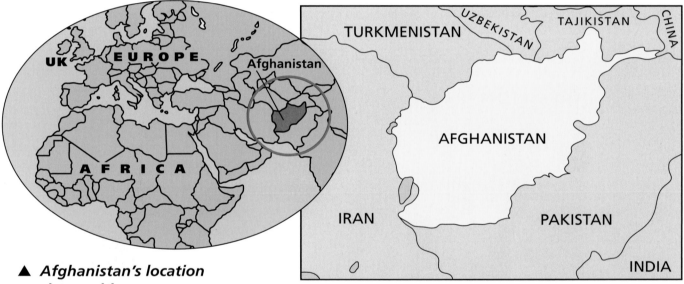

▲ *Afghanistan's location on the world map.*

▲ *Afghanistan lies between the countries of Central Asia and Pakistan. It borders Iran to the west and China to the east. Much of the land is taken up by high mountains, remote river valleys and harsh deserts. The climate is very hot in summer and bitterly cold in winter.*

To understand today's crisis we need to take a look at the land and its history. Afghanistan is a very poor country, with no access to the sea. One reason for its poverty is that its high mountains, deserts and harsh climate have always made it difficult to grow crops, and difficult to travel or to build roads. However, the country's central position at the crossroads of Asia did mean that important historical trading routes followed the rocky passes and valleys.

Afghanistan was not really considered to be a single country before 1747, but rather a series of separate homelands. It is still home to many different ethnic groups, including the Pashtun, Hazara, Tajik, Uzbek, Turkmen, Baluchi and Aimaq. This gathering of peoples has produced a rich variety of cultures but also divisions and conflicts that make it hard to unite the country even today. Many ethnic groups, such as the Pashtun, Uzbeks and Tajiks, extend beyond the Afghan border into other lands. This means that other countries often become entangled in Afghan politics.

Ancient invasions

Invading armies passed this way, time after time. About 2,500 years ago the Afghan region was part of a vast empire ruled by Persia (modern Iran). This was conquered by the great Macedonian general Alexander the Great, whose Greek army invaded Afghanistan in 330 BCE. Long after Alexander's empire had fallen, Greek cultural influences remained, mixing with Indian and other Asian cultures. The Buddhist faith took root here and thrived until the arrival of Islam in 652 CE.

Over the centuries, invaders of Afghanistan included Turks, Persians and Mongols, and their descendants the Mughals, Uzbeks and Persians. Rebellions were frequent and fierce. The Afridis, a Pashtun tribe, massacred a whole Mughal army in 1672.

The Great Game

In the 1700s and 1800s powerful European nations were competing to build global empires. The British beat the French in their bid to control Mughal India. The Russians took over the lands of Central Asia. Lying between the Northwest Frontier of British India and the growing Russian empire lay Afghanistan. Both the British and the Russians tried to gain control of this country and its rulers, through warfare and politics. One British spy executed in Central Asia in 1842 called this the "Great Game."

▲ *Giant statues of the Buddha were carved into cliffs at Bamiyan in the 500s CE. In 2001 they were blown up by the Taliban government for being "un-Islamic."*

Wars with the British Empire

The death of British soldiers in Afghanistan is nothing new. In 1839 the British invaded. In 1842 a whole British and Indian force numbering about 4,500 was slaughtered as they tried to withdraw southwards to India. The Afghans offered fierce resistance to the British again in 1878, but lost territory. In 1885 the Russians won land in the north of the country. The British were fighting the Afghans again in 1919. Not until 1921 was Afghanistan finally recognized as an independent nation.

The Cold War

There followed a period of violent struggles for power. In 1933 a new king was crowned, Muhammad Zahir Shah. During his long reign the British pulled out of India, and in 1947 a new state called Pakistan was created on Afghanistan's southeastern border. Another period of great international tension, rather like the Great Game of the 1800s, began in the 1950s. It was called the Cold War. The United States of America, Britain and other Western powers were competing with the communist Soviet Union (Russia).

A communist party (the PDPA or People's Democratic Party of Afghanistan) was founded in Afghanistan in 1965. In 1973 the army overthrew the king, and there followed another period of unrest and political killings. The PDPA now came to power, with a secular (nonreligious) program focused on land reform and literacy. Conservative and religious forces fiercely opposed them.

Fighting the Russians

In 1979 the Soviet Union invaded Afghanistan and installed a pro-Russian president named Babrak Karmal, who was replaced in 1987 by Mohammad Najibullah. The Russians wanted to make sure that Afghanistan remained pro-Soviet, but they had another worry, too. Iran had recently had a revolution that had brought Islamic fundamentalists to power. The Russians feared that this religious and political unrest could spread to their own Central Asian territories.

The invaders were soon caught up in a long war of resistance, which eventually killed tens of thousands of their troops. Perhaps a million Afghans died during this occupation. Many others fled from the fighting, ending up in refugee camps in Pakistan or Iran.

The Russians' opponents were known as the Mujahideen. They included irregular fighters belonging to various Islamic factions. They were joined by international Muslim fighters who shared their aims, and by warlords, powerful regional bosses or leaders of ethnic minorities who had their own militias. The anticommunist Mujahideen were funded, trained and armed with the support of the United States, Britain, Pakistan and Saudi Arabia, who all wanted to reduce the power of the Soviet Union.

They succeeded. The Russian troops withdrew in 1989. Their defeat played some part in the final downfall of the communist government in Russia. This resulted in the creation of new independent republics in Central Asia, on Afghanistan's northern border. The pro-Russian Najibullah government fell in 1992. The Mujahideen captured Kabul, and there was a civil war.

Case Study

▲ *In 1880 British troops were defeated at Maiwand.*

Then as now?

We know what people said and wrote about the Afghan wars of the 1800s — and a lot of it was remarkably similar to what people are saying and writing today.

A British poet named Rudyard Kipling (1865–1936, better known as author of *The Jungle Book*) wrote about Afghanistan and the Battle of Maiwand. He is widely remembered as a poet who was inspired by the British Empire, but he was always concerned about the conditions of the troops. He sometimes wrote in the harsh, non-heroic language of the common soldier:

"When you're wounded and left on Afghanistan's plains,
And the women come out to cut up what remains,
Jest roll to your rifle and blow out your brains,
An' go to your Gawd like a soldier."

Kipling was horrified by the waste of young life and prospects — an officer whose education had been expensive could be killed "like a rabbit" by a muzzle-loading rifle that cost only 10 rupees. He called this "the arithmetic on the Frontier."

Rise of the Taliban

In 1996 a Muslim militia known as the Taliban (meaning "religious students") captured the capital and set up government as the Islamic Emirate of Afghanistan. They were supported by Pakistan. The new government did not control the whole country, and had to fight an ongoing rebellion by a coalition called the United Islamic Front, or the Northern Alliance. This was made up of regional militia commanders or warlords, including many non-Pashtuns. Both sides committed atrocities during this bitter phase of the conflict.

The Taliban government was at first welcomed for bringing back order to a lawless state. However, their approach was puritanical and fundamentalist. They governed with a very harsh interpretation of traditional religious Islamic law, or Shari'a. There were public executions, floggings and even stonings. The few rights already enjoyed by women were withdrawn. Female education was banned, the daily movement of women outside the home was limited and in public women had to wear the traditional burqa, a robe covering the entire body with only a mesh panel through which to see. Men had to wear beards. Music and television were banned.

9/11 and after

On September 11, 2001, (also known as 9/11) a series of horrific terrorist attacks took place in the US, killing nearly 3,000 people. Hijacked aircraft were driven into the Twin Towers of the World Trade Center in New York City. Most of the terrorists were Saudi Arabians. None were Afghans. However it was reported that the

▲ *Osama bin Laden (1957–2011) was the mastermind behind 9/11.*

attack had been organized by a rich Saudi Arabian named Osama bin Laden, who had fought against the Russians with the Afghan Mujahideen. He had set up a secret terrorist organization called al Qaeda ("the base"), which operated from Afghanistan and aimed to attack "enemies of Islam" worldwide.

The US government demanded that the Taliban government hand over bin Laden to the Americans. The Taliban refused. In response, British and US planes bombed Afghanistan. Western forces helped the Northern Alliance to capture Kabul in December 2001. The Taliban government fell. With the backing of the United Nations (UN), an International Security Assistance Force (ISAF) was created, a military task force aiming to bring in stable government and reconstruction. Its troops have come at times from a total of 48 countries around the world, including the US, Canada, Australia, New Zealand, the UK and many other European nations. Command of the force later passed to NATO (the North Atlantic Treaty Organization). ISAF gradually extended its operation through the whole country, but met increasingly fierce opposition and high casualties, especially in the south and southeast. Their opponents included the Taliban and 11 other insurgent groups.

An international conference paved the way for a series of assemblies, leading to full presidential and parliamentary elections.

▼ *Different worlds – Afghan youths watch a Canadian soldier.*

Afghanistan today

Name: Islamic Republic of Afghanistan

Capital: Kabul

Major cities: Kandahar, Herat, Jalalabad, Mazar-e-Sharif

Area: 251,827 square miles (652,230 square kilometers)

Population: 29,121,286

Religions: Sunni Islam 80 percent; Shi'a Islam 19 percent; other 1 percent

Average adult literacy: Men 43 percent; women 13 percent

Workforce: Agriculture 78 percent; industry 6 percent; services 16 percent

Resources: Natural gas, coal, precious stones, copper

Products: hides, textiles, carpets, cement

Chapter 3

Waging war

Why are there over 350,000 international and Afghan government soldiers fighting in Afghanistan in 2011? How long are the foreign troops likely to remain there? The attack of 9/11 was the reason the Western powers went to war – but what did their governments aim to achieve? During the course of the conflict, the Western powers declared various political aims.

What are they fighting for?

The original plan of President George W. Bush was to overthrow the Taliban government in Afghanistan. This was achieved rapidly, in December 2001.

Another principal aim was to hunt down Osama bin Laden. Hiding places such as the remote Tora Bora caves near the Afghan border were bombed, but to no avail. The al Qaeda leader was not tracked down for another ten years. He was finally shot by US troops in Pakistan in May 2011.

By then al Qaeda networks had also appeared in other countries, such as Yemen. The future of the organization today remains unclear.

Another stated aim of the Western powers when they entered Afghanistan was to make the country safe for reconstruction. Many billions of dollars from the US and dozens of other countries have indeed been spent on aid. However the work has been hampered by fraud, waste and inefficiency.

▲ *The search for bin Laden – US bombs pound the caves at Tora Bora in 2001.*

Viewpoints

"I think we need to just be very clear about what we're trying to do in Afghanistan. Frankly, we're not trying to create the perfect democracy. We're never going to create some ideal society. We are simply there for our own national security."

David Cameron, British Prime Minister, 2010

"There is a clear and pressing need to end the monumental folly of prosecuting a war in Afghanistan... The war ... is the rallying cause for terrorist acts against civilian targets across the world."

Editorial, the *Guardian* newspaper, 2010

▲ *US Marines carry a wounded comrade after a roadside bomb hit their vehicle in 2010 in Helmand Province.*

• Is waging war an effective way of preventing future terrorism in other countries? Or does the war just create new enemies?

Reconstruction has also been set back by continuous fighting and the lack of security for aid workers.

Another reason for the military operations was to allow a stable, democratic government to function. Elections have been held, although there have been accusations of vote rigging and intimidation. The government of Hamid Karzai has been accused of corruption, and there have been increasing tensions between Karzai and the United States government.

Many politicians and NATO generals say that the chief aim of this war has been to prevent further terrorist attacks on the streets of New York, London or other western cities.

The description of the Afghan war as part of a wider "war on terror" was first raised by President George W. Bush in 2001. It was later extended to include the invasion and occupation of Iraq, which started in 2003, and many other military or secret operations. The term found favor with much of the Western press and supporters of the war.

The notion of a "war on terror" has been used to justify extraordinary measures, such as the indefinite detention of military prisoners in camps at Guantánamo Bay, a US naval base on the island of Cuba, without due legal process. This means that suspected terrorists have been held without charge or trial.

A war on terror?

Just what was meant by the phrase "war on terror"? "Terrorism" is a not a precise legal term, and "terror" even less so. In 2009 the US Department of defense replaced the official term "Global War on Terror" with another vague but less controversial term – this was now an "Overseas Contingency Operation."

▲ *The battle for Nawzad lasted for three long years, from 2006 to 2009.*

Terrorist outrages have been common around the world during the course of this war. On July 7, 2005 four bombers murdered 52 people and injured about 700 in London. The war in Afghanistan had not prevented this attack. Has it prevented others?

Critics of the war claim that the war has actually made international terrorist attacks more likely. They point out that many Muslims around the world resent the presence of western troops in Afghanistan and are angered by reports of civilian casualties there and across the border in Pakistan. They say many young Muslims become radicalized in the first place by watching the news.

If al Qaeda is no longer based in Afghanistan, is this war even being fought in the right place? Is the problem now what is happening in Pakistan or Yemen?

Plans and strategy

Western governments made the political decision to go to war, but it was the army generals of NATO who had to win that war. Could it be done? And which of their objectives were to be achieved? How would it be possible to win the hearts and minds of ordinary Afghans, when innocent civilians were being killed by ISAF troops? Would the Afghan government forces be capable of taking over responsibility for security?

During this conflict there have been repeated tensions between the US and UK governments, and their military commanders. Many issues have become public or media debates. How many troops were required on the ground? Did the 2003 invasion of Iraq divert the resources needed to win the Afghan war? Were the soldiers properly equipped and armed? Were their conditions of service and medical treatment adequate? How could communications between the various allied forces be improved to avoid casualties through friendly fire?

What was to be done about insurgents who crossed the remote, mountainous borders into Pakistan, only to regroup and return? One decision was made in 2004, when the US decided to attack Taliban bases in Pakistan with unmanned, remote-controlled aircraft called drones. These attacks continue today. They are said to have killed some prominent militants, but there have also been many civilian casualties, and this has created a political crisis in Pakistan. Questions have also been raised about whether killing suspects in this way is simply a form of assassination without legal process, and whether it is valid under international law.

A second strategy was adopted in 2009, when the Pakistani army attacked the Taliban strongholds in their own country. This forced many civilians to flee the region as refugees, and critics argued that the military gains were temporary.

Case Study

Marine pallbearers carry the flag-draped coffin of a Marine who was killed in Afghanistan in February 2011.

The Afghanistan "surge"

Starting in December 2009, U.S. President Barack Obama increased the war effort dramatically. The process began under U.S. General Stanley McChrystal and continued after General David Petraeus took command of NATO forces in Afghanistan in July 2010. The month of January 2011 saw deployment of special operations forces, increased use of tanks and missiles, a doubling of bombing raids and hundreds more surveillance missions using manned aircraft or drones.

The plan, previously tried by General Petraeus in Iraq, was to create a 'surge' offensive, with the aim of reducing violent resistance and so make a political solution more likely. In all, the surge added more than 30,000 US troops to Afghanistan, bringing the total number of US forces to 100,000. In June 2011, President Obama announced plans for a drawdown. The plan was to withdraw all surge troops in 2012 and the remainder of US troops by 2014. Critics have raised concern about the readiness of Afghan government troops to take over.

The media

Media management is also an important part of military strategy. Journalists are often embedded within ISAF forces to encourage favorable news coverage. Some say that military commanders tend to present optimistic assessments of their progress in order to bring public opinion on their side and keep up the morale of their troops. Their views may be challenged or contradicted by politicians, diplomats, journalists or bloggers.

There are now contacts being made between the international forces and elements of the Taliban, suggesting that a compromise is being considered. Is that to be expected? Is it to be seen as a success or as a failure of strategy? It is hard for the public to make judgments, when Afghanistan is so distant and so different from the world they are familiar with, and when they must sort out the truth from the propaganda.

The war on the ground

The wider questions of politics and strategy, such as troop numbers and supplies, affect the soldiers of ISAF on the ground every day. The everyday conditions and morale of ordinary soldiers will also affect the outcome. These men and women are professional soldiers, not conscripts. They may face sniper fire or the hidden homemade bombs known as IEDs (improvised explosive devices). They may risk their lives whenever they go on patrol or enter a building. They have to endure extreme heat or cold, or dust storms. They often show great bravery in bomb disposal, in rescuing injured troops or landing helicopters. The reality of battle is often grim, and may cause physical injuries or mental stress, which last long after service is completed, affecting health, work or family life.

The insurgents fight the same battles in the same conditions, but lack the same degree of military equipment, aircraft, communications and medical support. They are up against some of the most powerful armies in the world. Their military advantage lies in detailed local knowledge and in having time on their side. The ISAF forces will have to withdraw at some point, whereas Afghan government forces and insurgents are there for the long term.

Suffering of civilians

The overthrow of the Taliban in 2001 benefitted Afghanistan's civilian population, for example in improving the opportunities for women, but this long war has brought suffering as well. Many civilians, including women and children, have been killed accidentally in bombing raids by ISAF forces. IEDs left by the insurgents killed 690 civilians in 2010. Other civilians were killed by suicide bombings in public places or in revenge killings by militias. Through 2010 between six and seven civilians were being killed every day in Afghanistan, and eight or nine wounded.

Tens of thousands of civilians have been caught in the fighting between the two sides and driven from their homes. They have suffered intimidation from insurgents and warlords, economic problems and lack of security. Add these problems to disease, hunger and poverty, and one can see why on average Afghan men and women can only expect to live to the age of 45. Twenty percent of all children die before their fifth birthday. After many decades of warfare, about three million Afghans are still refugees living in other lands.

All those involved in or affected by this conflict need a peaceful future. How can it be brought about?

Viewpoints:

"Some of the generals are saying, 'We're making progress. We are clearing an area.' But you really don't defeat the Taliban by clearing an area. They move."

Colin Powell, US statesman and retired general

"I will go back [to the US] convinced that our strategy is working and that we will be able to achieve key goals."

Robert Gates, US Secretary of Defense

• When two regular armies are fighting each other in pitched battles, it is fairly clear who is winning and who is losing. When an army is attacking irregular fighters over a large area, it is harder to foresee the likely outcome.

• These two US officials see the progress in Afghanistan differently. What factors might have led to their different views?

A group of Taliban fighters gathers.

Chapter 4

Politics, faith and power

People on all sides of the Afghanistan war agree that there can be no lasting peace in Afghanistan without a stable government, although they do not necessarily agree on what kind of government that should be. Should it be a Western-style democracy? Should it be secular, or based on traditional Islamic law, the Shari'a? Should it include traditional assemblies such as the councils of the Pashtun people, Afghanistan's majority ethnic group?

After the Taliban

The present system of government was introduced by a process that began with an international conference held at Bonn, Germany, in 2001, with the support of the United Nations. The conference appointed Hamid Karzai, a Pashtun from Kandahar with family connections in the US, as temporary president. In 2002 an appointed council or Loya Jirga of leading Afghan figures confirmed Karzai as leader. He was finally voted in by the public as president in 2004. In the following year Afghanistan had its first democratic parliamentary elections in 30 years.

The constitution and parliament

Afghanistan's constitution was drawn up in 2003, following the same political process. A constitution is the legal framework that sets out how a country is to be governed and how it makes its laws.

The president is directly elected for a five-year term. The National Assembly has two chambers. The Wolesi Jirga is the elected parliament, with members representing regions. Sixty-eight of its total of 250 seats are reserved for women. The second chamber is the Meshrano Jirga. It is made

▲ *This photograph shows Afghanistan's elected parliament in session.*

up of 120 important people elected by regional councils or appointed by the president, and its job is to approve or revise legislation.

Democracy in action?

At the moment there are seven major political parties in Afghanistan, and thirteen smaller ones. The Taliban is banned as a political party, and so is the Communist Party of Afghanistan.

The establishment of democracy in Afghanistan has not been easy. National Assembly members have included some controversial figures, former regional warlords or their supporters, some of them suspected of war crimes during the decades of fighting. There are members who are not known for their democratic ideals or their regard for human rights. Some of the women delegates are believed not to have been genuinely independent members, but proxies ordered to vote for the policies of the warlords.

Critics say that these issues have damaged the Assembly's credibility and efficiency. However supporters say that things cannot be changed overnight. It is better that the real powers in the country are in the debating chamber.

Viewpoints

"The Afghan people dared rockets, bombs and intimidation and came out to vote."

Hamid Karzai, President of Afghanistan, on the 2009 presidential election

"If we allow he who robbed the votes of this country to move forward, we would give the Afghan people a future that they do not want to see, and I think this goes also for the international community."

Abdullah Abdullah, rival candidate in the 2009 presidential election

"Neither the US nor jihadis and Taliban! Long live the struggle of independent and democratic forces of Afghanistan!"

Slogan of the Revolutionary Association of the Women of Afghanistan (RAWA), 2008

• While Karzai and Abdullah argued about the result of the 2009 presidential election, many Afghans wanted more radical change and an end to corruption. Afghan women founded RAWA in 1977 to promote human rights and secular democracy. RAWA fought the Soviet invasion. It has opposed rule by warlords, rule by the Taliban, the international military presence and rule by the Karzai government.

▲ *Hamid Karzai has been elected Afghan president twice.*

The elections in 2004 and 2005 were not perfect, but they gave hope to many ordinary people in Afghanistan and were welcomed by many international governments as a major step towards peace and democracy.

Sadly, the 2009 presidential election, costing hundreds of millions of dollars, was marked by increased fraud, violence and intimidation. Over 2,800 complaints were made, and 1.26 million votes were thrown out. Even the electoral commission was accused of being corrupt. A runoff election had to be held between Hamid Karzai and his political opponent Abdullah Abdullah. It was won by Karzai.

The 2010 general election was delayed, and it saw a further increase in complaints. Twenty percent of the votes were declared void and twenty-one candidates disqualified. The turnout was only 36 percent of the electorate. The Taliban tried to intimidate people from voting. Fourteen people were killed on election day. Some say the fact that the election took place at all was a significant achievement.

Corruption and efficiency

Security and flawed elections are clearly major obstacles to lasting peace, justice and prosperity in Afghanistan. An equally great danger comes from corruption in everyday life, with government officials and police regularly taking bribes. That is nothing

▲ *Abdullah Abdullah speaks at a press conference in Kabul in 2009.*

new in Afghanistan's history, but without effective government and rule of law, little can be achieved to improve people's lives. There are many people in Afghanistan determined to do just that, and the future will rely on them winning support and being elected.

▲ *Women vote in September 2010.*

Religion and the law

Afghanistan is an Islamic Republic. Its constitution declares that the president has to be a Muslim, that Islam is the established religion and that no law may contradict the teachings of Islam.

Afghanistan civil law is partly based on an Islamic legal code known as Hanafi. Laws for the Shi'a Muslim minority are based upon a stricter form of Shari'a. Afghan justice has generally moved away from the extreme and often cruel punishments used by the Taliban, but these may still occur in parts of Afghanistan where Taliban insurgents have control, or where government power is weak. In 2010 a couple was stoned to death in the northern Kunduz province, and a pregnant woman was lashed and killed in Baghdis in the east. Some Afghans still respect Taliban justice for its speed and effectiveness in halting crime, but others reject it for breaching the most basic human rights, and they fear its return.

Viewpoints:

"GETTING SERIOUS ABOUT TACKLING CORRUPTION: AFGHAN ATTORNEY-GENERAL TO INDICT FIVE LEADING POLITICANS."

Headline, Spiegel Online, November 2009

"My cousin runs a medical practice [in Afghanistan]. Some expired and low-quality drugs were found in his clinic and the health department started a procedure to take him to court. Later, he bribed the head doctor and his file was clean within a day. My cousin is still selling the expired and poor-quality drugs..."

UNDOC (United Nations Office on Drugs and Crime), evidence given to a survey in 2010

• Corruption in Afghanistan has occured on a massive scale. In 2009 the *Washington Post* newspaper reported that an Afghan government mining minister took $30 million in bribes on just one contract. However, it is often the small, everyday bribing and corruption that drives ordinary people to despair. Future politicians will need to come to grips with this problem if the country is to make a fresh start.

Politics and religion

Politics and religion are closely linked in Afghanistan. Before the 2009 presidential election, Hamid Karzai tried to win conservative support among leaders of the Shi'a Muslim minority by supporting legislation that severely restricted the rights of Shi'a women. Afghan women protested on the streets, and Karzai was strongly criticized by Western governments and human rights groups for this move.

Regional power

Another political problem also has a long history in Afghanistan. This is the inability of governments in Kabul to be effective across the whole country. The nation has always been divided by the geography of its mountain ranges and valleys, as well as by the ethnic, cultural and religious divisions of the population. This has resulted in regional leaders seizing too much personal power and believing themselves to be above the law. Some are corrupt or criminal, some may be former warlords, running their own militias. Political leaders in Afghanistan have to form regional alliances in order to be elected but in the process may lay themselves open to criticism for their choice of political allies.

Crossing borders

The political problems of Afghanistan would be difficult enough to solve if the country stood on its own. But it does not. It is at the center of a whole region that is troubled by political crises. Solving Afghanistan's problems is like trying to unravel a mass of knots, whose strings are attached to other lands.

These international connections make Afghanistan's problems even harder to solve, and make it of the greatest importance to the whole world that a solution is found.

Case Study

The man from the Panjshir Valley

Mohammad Qasim Fahim (b.1957) is a Tajik from the Panjshir Valley region of north central Afghanistan, on the edge of the Hindu Kush Mountains. He belongs to the Jamiat-e Islami party.

Afghanistan and Iran

Iran has much shared history with Afghanistan. Millions of Afghan refugees have fled over the Iran border during years of conflict. The Dari language, spoken in western Afghanistan, is a form of the Persian language, which is spoken in Iran. Both countries are Muslim, but only 19 percent of Afghans follow the same form of the faith, Shi'a, as the Iranians. Iran was opposed to the original Taliban government, which belonged to the Sunni branch of Islam. Iran took part in the Bonn conference, which set up the new constitution in Afghanistan. It has also provided aid to fund new road projects in Afghanistan.

◄ *Afghan President Hamid Karzai (left) walks with First Vice President Mohammad Qasim Fahim in Kabul in March 2010.*

Fahim became effective leader of the Northern Alliance forces, which marched into Kabul in November 2001. He was made Minister of Defense in the temporary government that followed, but retained a personal militia, complete with tanks and missiles, until December 2003. He survived several assassination attempts.

Although Fahim is said to have once arrested and interrogated Hamid Karzai during the 1990s, in 2006 Karzai insisted that Fahim was respectable, a "dear friend" and "brother". He chose him as running mate in the 2009 presidential election although his opponents said that Fahim was engaged in criminal activities. To the dismay of human rights campaigners, Mohammad Qasim Fahim became First Vice President of Afghanistan. In 2010 he called for an assembly to negotiate with the insurgents.

Fahim fought with the Mujahideen against the Soviet invaders, and he stands accused by the organization Human Rights Watch of having been commander of the forces that carried out the Afshar massacre in Kabul in 1992. This involved rape, looting and the murder of some 800 Hazara people.

Iranian arms

Iran is also engaged in a bitter power struggle with the US, and claims have been made that Iran is funding its former enemy, the Taliban, and smuggling explosives across the border. Many observers believe that such involvement does exist, but at a low level. They say that Iran wants to speed up the exit of international forces from Iran, but needs good relations in the future with a stable government in Kabul. The Iranian government strongly denies any support for the insurgents.

The Pakistan connection

Pakistan has even closer links with Afghanistan. The Pashtun people of south and southeastern Afghanistan also live across the Pakistan border. Pakistan sponsored the fight of the Mujahideen against the Russians in the 1980s, and took in three million or more Afghan refugees. It supported the rise of the Taliban.

Today, Pakistan is an ally of the United States, receiving over $1 billion a year to fight militants on its own side of the border. Their bases harbor insurgents who cross the border to fight in Afghanistan. Pakistan has had nuclear weapons since 1998 and has very strained relations with its neighbor India, another nuclear power. Any instability in Pakistan could have very serious consequences for all of Asia, and for the rest of the world.

Pipeline politics

China, the world's biggest nation, shares a border of only 47 miles (76 km) with Afghanistan. However, it, too, shares ethnic links with groups such as the Tajiks. Having the world's fastest growing economy, China has a very strong interest in the economy and the resources of Central Asia. Russia also shares these economic interests, as well as concern over the role of militant Islam in the conflict in its own Caucasus region.

The Central Asian republics (Turkmenistan, Uzbekistan and Tajikistan) are also part of the bigger political equation. They have close ethnic links across Afghanistan's northern borders. They are important access points for supplies and military equipment as long as the war continues. They also have great importance for their natural gas resources and the routing of pipelines.

The US has long wanted to support the construction of a Trans-Afghanistan Pipeline (TAP) for natural gas from the Caspian Sea region across Turkmenistan, Afghanistan

▲ *This killer drone over Pakistan is remotely controlled from the US.*

and Pakistan, rather than through Russia, China or Iran. Some people believe that pipeline politics was always a major reason for this war. The Afghan pipeline route was opposed by the Taliban, but Karzai supports the project. It would seem that the Great Game is far from over even today. At home and abroad, the road to peace in Afghanistan is full of dangers and difficulties.

▲ *A new Great Game? US President Obama signs a deal with Russian President Medvedev in 2010.*

Viewpoints:

"If they don't stop [interfering in Afghanistan], the consequences will be ... that the region will suffer with us equally. All the countries in the neighborhood have the same ethnic groups that we have..."

Hamid Karzai, President of Afghanistan, February 2006

"We are very hopeful that our brother nation of Iran will work with us in bringing peace and security to Afghanistan so that both our countries will be secure."

Hamid Karzai, President of Afghanistan, March 2010, Reuters online press report June 2010

• Afghanistan must have good relations with its neighbors to secure a peaceful future. However they all have their own political and economic agendas when it comes to Afghanistan.

Chapter 5

Economics and aid

Without a flourishing, self-reliant economy in the future, Afghanistan is unlikely to enjoy peace or stability. At the moment, growing up in Afghanistan can be tough. The provision of housing, water supplies and electricity is very poor. There is a lack of health care, and the standard of living is very low.

Education may have been extended to include girls since the days of Taliban rule, but schools are often run-down and overcrowded, and pupils must struggle for books and the most basic resources. The US development agency, USAID, estimates that over six million Afghans (from a population of around 29 million) do not have enough food to eat.

▲ *Poverty prevents social progress.*

Work and resources

There are very limited opportunities for jobs for young Afghans upon leaving school. Most people live by farming, yet only 12 percent of the land is suitable for cultivation. Natural forests have been cut down for firewood, and so soils have become eroded and dry, turning into desert during years of drought.

Exports from Afghanistan include fruits, such as apricots and pomegranates, and nuts, such as walnuts, pistachios and almonds. Many people are herders, and sheepskin and hides are exported as well as magnificent traditional carpets made from the wool. Gemstones such as lapis lazuli have been mined for thousands of years, but the modern development of other resources, such as natural gas and copper, has been delayed by the long years of conflict. However, these resources do promise future wealth.

Trading in opium

Some of Afghanistan's trading is the illegal and highly profitable export of addictive drugs. The country is the world's largest producer of both hashish and opium. The opium poppy thrives in this climate. It can be processed to make the painkiller morphine as well as the drug heroin, which causes so much misery and crime around the world. In 2000 the Taliban government banned opium production, and extreme punishments brought dramatic results. The US paid the Taliban government $43 million for carrying out this program.

Viewpoints:

"Afghanistan... has enough natural resources to provide the basis of a sustainable economy that would be an alternative to a drug economy."

Ashraf Ghani, formerly Afghan Minister of Finance, April 2009

"When you see more conflict, when you see more poverty, you will see more opium cultivation."

Jean Luc Lemahieu, United Nations Office on Drugs and Crime (UNODC), 2011

• War, crime and poverty encourage poor farmers to grow opium poppies. But these problems also hinder industrial development, which is needed to transform the Afghan economy.

▼ *Troops burn opium in 2007.*

After 2001, the agreed government policy continued to be to ban opium, to destroy crops, to enforce the law and to provide farmers with an alternative income or different crops, such as wheat. Despite this, opium production soared. For many poor farmers, the opium poppy remained the only crop that brought in good profits. Big money also flowed back to criminals, to local warlords and militias, to Taliban fighters and corrupt government officials. To the troops, facing a growing insurgency, the destruction of the opium crop was not a priority, and risked making too many enemies.

However some antidrug actions have continued, and in 2010 these even included, for the first time, cooperation between NATO and its old enemy, the Russians. A fungus outbreak in that same year attacked the poppy crop, causing a 48 percent drop in opium production. Many farmers in Afghanistan believed this plant disease has been spread by US agents. Some observers claim it has been developed in Uzbekistan with Western funding, and they fear that it might do wider environmental harm. Even so, some experts believe opium production will recover and increase in 2011.

Rebuilding the country

The urgent need to tackle Afghan poverty and rebuild the country's infrastructure was realized from the outset of the current conflict. In 2002 and during the years since, international conferences have pledged aid worth over $67 billion. Unfortunately, many pledges were not fulfilled. Billions of dollars' worth of aid went missing, due to bureaucracy or corruption. Even so, aid that has been received has begun to improve the Afghan economy and help trade. In many areas, markets are busy once again, and the rapid spread of electronic media and mobile phones has transformed communications.

International aid

Hundreds of international aid agencies, government bodies and other NGOs (non-governmental organizations) have been working in Afghanistan in recent years. They have built roads and dams and worked on agricultural and tree-planting projects, and on health and education.

However, different agencies have had different policies. Some have wanted big business to step in. Others have wanted to concentrate on long-term development in poor rural areas. Critics have complained of a lack of coordination between agencies, and of too much money going to pay Western NGO managers and officials. Perhaps the main problem has been security. Violence and continuing warfare has led to some confusion between the role of the military and the role of civilian agencies. Project volunteers have been kidnapped and killed. International workers have had to be withdrawn from certain regions for their own safety, and this has limited the amount of reconstruction that has been possible.

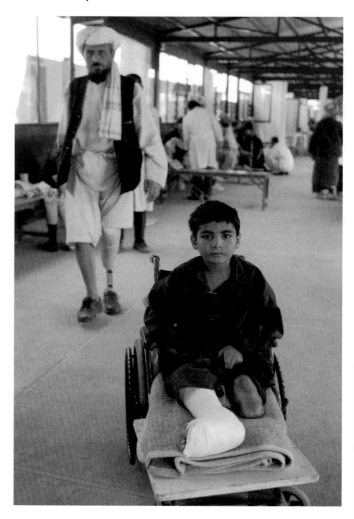

▲ *This young boy was injured by a land mine. He is being cared for by the Red Cross in Kabul.*

Case Study

Planting for the future

▲ *Newly planted walnut saplings benefit from the irrigation aid in Afghanistan.*

Practical help towards Afghanistan's future has been given by the United Nations Office for Project Services (UNOPS). Using US funding and working together with the Afghanistan government, this agency set up an Afghanistan Conservation Corps (ACC) to work right across the country. Its workers have planted millions of trees for forestry and fruit production, tackled soil erosion and water conservation and taught rural communities about scientific methods of managing the environment. They have trained thousands of people to be workers and teachers. The protection of the natural environment is crucial in a nation in which the great majority of the population live in rural areas, with 80 percent of these people depending on these natural resources for their work.

Chapter 6
Human rights

Some of the main issues to arise from the Afghan war have centered on abuses of human rights. Although human rights were not the original reason for going to war, the West's criticism of Taliban rule placed great emphasis on their legal system, their harsh punishments and their treatment of women and girls.

What are human rights?

Over the ages, societies around the world developed their own codes of morality and ethics. These were often based on religious or social customs. They described the way in which people should treat each other. They had much in common, for example, in condemning acts such as murder or theft. In the 1600s and 1700s, thinkers tried to work out how society should be organized if most people were to lead a happy and healthy life. They listed basic needs such as liberty, justice, freedom from oppression and poverty, equality, fair working conditions, freedom of movement or free speech.

Are rights universal?

In 1948 the United Nations drew up a Universal Declaration of Human Rights. These rights were intended to be valid in all nations, societies and cultures at all times. However, even before the rise of the Taliban, many Afghans lived according to ancient tribal customs or religious traditions, which were often very different from the ideals of the United Nations. In Afghan society men have generally held the power and the rights of women to move freely, to dress freely, to be educated and employed, have been restricted.

Under the Taliban government, human rights abuses extended to political rights, freedom of speech, freedom of worship, imprisonment and punishment and discrimination against ethnic minorities. Public hangings, stoning to death and lashing were common.

Such differences between the ideals of the United Nations and the traditional practices in a particular region or nation raise many questions. Are human rights really universal, or are they relative to history and culture? Can human rights be imposed by one group of people on another, or do they have to evolve naturally? The debate is worth having, but perhaps what counts most is people's practical experience of what happens to them day to day. Are people suffering?

In Afghanistan today

There is no doubt that human rights for Afghans have improved in many ways since 2001. Today 57 percent of girls go to school or college. Women may work in health care or the legal system. Some women serve as members of the parliament, the Wolesi Jirga. These reforms mark great advances, despite their limitations. There are more political freedoms and more small pleasures in daily life, such as being able to listen to music or watch films.

Viewpoints:

"Everyone has the right to freedom of peaceful assembly and association."

United Nations Universal Declaration of Human Rights (UDHR), Article 20.1

• The ideals expressed in the UDHR are still a long way from being realized in Afghanistan, although progress has clearly been made. To what extent do Western perceptions color human international rights campaigns?

▼ *Should there be school or work for poor Afghan children?*

"The shooting of a female Afghan politician... demonstrates the fragility of the modest gains made by Afghan women after the fall of the Taliban.... Nada Khan, a female Provincial Council member, was left in critical condition after being attacked in a drive-by shooting in Pul-e-Khumri, the provincial capital of Baghlan in northern Afghanistan."

Amnesty International report, April 2010

The rights of women

Despite improvements, rape and violence against women are still common in many parts of Afghan society. Most girls are married off before they are 16, sometimes to older men or for money. If they flee an arranged marriage they risk being attacked, or even arrested on trumped-up charges.

Child abuse of boys and girls, under-age working and lack of education are common. Schools are often burned down and teachers threatened or killed. There is also concern about the current treatment of prisoners in Afghan jails.

▼ *Afghanistan's three million nomads have suffered greatly from warfare, drought and ethnic conflict.*

Restrictions on free speech were eased in 2004, but journalists are still threatened. The communications media are mostly state owned.

Afghan activists point out that the continuing war and lack of security affect the human rights of women and children every bit as much as government or Taliban policy. Fighting may make it impossible for women to leave the home or take a job anyway, and violent crime and corruption may make life unbearable.

Many feel that they cannot win. On the one hand, the fighting destroys their basic human rights, yet on the other they fear that if the war ends in a peace deal with conservative forces, then the old abuses will once more become official policy and any new improvements will be swept away.

Case Study

Malalai Joya speaks out

Malalai Joya was born in 1978 and raised in Afghan refugee camps in Iran and then Pakistan. Returning to her homeland in 1998, she worked with women's organizations in the western provinces of Farah and Herat.

As a delegate to a Loya Jirga, which was called to approve the new constitution in 2003, Joya caused uproar by accusing the assembly of being packed with former warlords and criminals. She was elected to the Wolesi Jirga in 2005, where she again accused those present of including in their midst many of the same old warlords, with pockets full of US dollars, pretending to be democratic. Joya infuriated her opponents and was suspended from the assembly in 2007. She did not stand in the 2010 election. Despite death threats, Joya has traveled the world to speak about the abuse of power and women's rights in Afghanistan.

▲ *Malalai Joya is surrounded by children at the Nahed Orphanage, Kabul, in 2007.*

Perhaps the most encouraging development in recent years is the growth of radical activist groups in Afghanistan who are prepared to stand up for their rights against all sides and all factions.

Extraordinary measures?

If human rights are to be honored universally, then everyone has a duty to observe them in all situations – including the Western powers. As the so-called War on Terror developed, the legal practices of the US were also called into question by international human rights organizations. At issue were the arrest and imprisonment of suspects, the treatment of prisoners and the lack of due legal process. Even today many prisoners are left in a legal limbo.

After 2001 the US government argued that extraordinary measures were necessary in extraordinary times. Their opponents argued that international law and human rights had to be upheld, especially in extraordinary times.

Detention and rendition

After the overthrow of the Taliban, large numbers of Afghans and people who were visiting or had visited Afghanistan were taken into detention by US forces. Some were suspected of involvement with Al Qaeda or the Taliban, or were seized on the word of paid informants. Some just happened to be in the wrong place at the wrong time. They were sent to prisons such as Bagram Internment Facility at an air base to the north of Kabul. There were accusations of prisoner abuse, torture and killings by the prison guards. Some low-ranking US soldiers were convicted, but they only received minor punishments.

As the "War on Terror" developed and spread, people of many different nationalities were seized in other parts of the world. They were detained in secret without due legal process, and outside the provisions of the Geneva Conventions, a series of international treaties that govern the treatment of prisoners of war. Some were secretly flown to prisons in other countries, where they were interrogated and sometimes tortured. This process became known as rendition.

The US government at that time disputed definitions of torture and claimed that useful intelligence was being gathered that would prevent terrorism and save lives. Critics insisted that methods such as waterboarding (partially drowning a prisoner) and sleep deprivation were a form of torture, and that intelligence gained under torture could not be regarded as reliable or be valid in a court of law.

Guantánamo Bay

From January 2002 more and more prisoners were taken in shackles to prison camps at Guantánamo Bay, a US base on the Caribbean island of Cuba. This base was at the time considered to lie outside the rule of US law. Detention was indefinite, in contradiction of the ancient legal principle known as habeas corpus, whereby a detained person has to be brought to trial. Prisoners were not told why they were being held. Claims of severe prisoner

Viewpoints:

abuse were supported by the International Committee of the Red Cross in a confidential report in 2004 but were rejected by the US government. Several prisoner suicides occured, and attempted suicides became common.

By 2011, 779 prisoners were recorded as having been held at Guantánamo, 221 of them Afghan citizens. It has become clear that many of them were innocent. When many detainees were eventually released, no charges were brought against them. Only

a few were brought to trial, and then some were brought before a military tribunal, not a full court of law. In 2009 President Obama announced that Guantánamo Bay would be closed down, but in February 2011 it remained in use with 173 prisoners still being held.

Can it be said that these operations were necessary? Many believe that they have damaged western claims to hold the moral high ground.

"I'm glad they're at Guantánamo. I don't want them on our soil. I want them on Guantánamo, where they don't get the access to lawyers..."

Mitt Romney, former Governor of Massachusetts, May 2007

"Those who would give up essential liberty to purchase a little temporary safety deserve neither liberty nor safety."

Benjamin Franklin, Historical Review of Pennsylvania (1759)

• Benjamin Franklin was one of the founding fathers of the United States. What would he have thought of Guantánamo Bay?

◄ *Detainees are herded into cages at Guantánamo Bay in 2002.*

Chapter 7

Hopes for the future

By 2011 the war in Afghanistan had lasted ten years. By comparison World War I lasted only four years (1914–18) and World War II only six years (1939–1945). Some generals and diplomats have said that the Western powers will need to remain in Afghanistan for perhaps 20 or even 30 years to see their work completed. Others say that the war is now being won, that one last push, one last "surge" will win the war. Historians remember similar pronouncements being repeated in vain during the 1960s, when America was fighting in Vietnam.

Can the war go on?

The longer options are not too realistic. It is hard to wage a war without popular backing at home. In 2010, only 7 percent of Britons thought more UK troops should be sent to Afghanistan. In the same year, 60 percent of Americans felt that this war

▲ *Kabul was devastated by fighting between rival Mujahideen factions in 1992. Afghanistan has a long history of unrest.*

was not worth fighting, even though leaders of mainstream political parties in the West were saying the opposite.

The war has little public support internationally. As early as 2007 an international opinion poll showed that in only two out of 47 countries did a majority of the public want international forces to remain in Afghanistan. Dutch forces pulled out of the war in 2010.

This war cost the United States $120 billion in 2010 alone. At a time of economic hardship around the world, the expense of the war is a major concern in the West.

Withdrawal?

Any timetable for withdrawal is a political necessity, but it also benefits the insurgents, who can play a waiting game. In November 2010 NATO agreed that security would be handed over to Afghan forces by 2014. International forces would, however, remain in the country after that to train and support the Afghan national army.

However, the presence of those troops would probably anger many Afghans and international fighters, encouraging further attacks or acts of terrorism.

Viewpoints

"Development aid is being abused in order to pursue military goals and to privatize the Afghan economy. The government must withdraw troops now and support a political solution under UN auspices [supervision]..."

The global poverty charity War on Want, UK, February 2011

"Hopefully, we will have totally turned over the ability to the Afghan security forces to maintain the security of the country...But we are not leaving if you do not want us to leave."

Joe Biden, US Vice President, January 2011

• Which policy will offer the quickest road to a lasting peace?

• Why do you think these writers hold different opinions about how long troops should stay in Afghanistan?

▶ *RAWA protestors demand peace and democracy in April 2007.*

Time for withdrawal?

Some activists believe that immediate withdrawal of NATO troops would bring peace sooner rather than later. They point out that at some point any resolution of the conflict will have to involve negotiations with the enemy.

Talking with the Taliban

In fact, informal contacts are already being made between the Afghan and international governments on one side and some elements of the Taliban on the other. Some politicians believe that the more moderate insurgents might be persuaded to drop some of the extreme policies of their past. Some Afghan politicians and also human rights activists see little hope of that.

Likewise, the Taliban find it difficult to trust their enemies, unless they first receive firm guarantees about their future.

Future security

Continuing conflict and lack of security would set back reconstruction and international aid work, and this really must continue for decades if Afghanistan is to have a peaceful future. If economic support for Afghanistan ends when the troops withdraw, there is trouble ahead.

The most important factor in ensuring a peaceful and secure Afghanistan is having a secure and democratic government that is not corrupt and that honors human rights.

A time for hope?

In 2009 there were popular protests in Iran against presidential election results. They were put down violently by the government. In 2011 a series of popular protests overthrew the governments of Tunisia and Egypt. It seems that in many countries ordinary people are demanding more democratic forms of government. But they also want to go their own way in the world without being manipulated by foreign governments, or becoming the victims of international rivalries about oil and gas reserves. Could this finally be the end of the Great Game of the 1800s?

▲ *ISAF and Afghan girls play a friendly soccer match in 2010. The Afghan women's team was founded in 2004 and played its first international match against Pakistan in 2007.*

Case Study

Coming home

During the wars of the 1980s and '90s, many Afghans fled abroad, mostly to camps in Iran and Pakistan. Over 2.5 million refugees remain outside Afghanistan's borders, where they must register with the authorities. Many are not welcome guests in their adopted country. Since 2002 over five million refugees have made the journey back to Afghanistan, encouraged by the offer of land and some immediate expenses for travel and food. The refugees are helped by the United Nations Refugee Agency (UNHCR). It is not always an easy journey, because of continuing conflict and violence. The return of refugees has increased the Afghan population by over 20 percent, and in poverty-stricken

▲ *Afghan refugees wait for their turn at the UNHCR registration center in Peshawar in April 2010. Around 1.7 million Afghan refugees remain in Pakistan after fleeing their homeland.*

areas this places a great strain on the local economy. Young returnees are at risk from violence and crime. Will a future Afghanistan be able to provide a safe and peaceful homeland for its scattered peoples?

A time for fear?

Whether these hopes are fulfilled in the Middle East is one thing. Whether reform and change can flourish farther east, in the mountains and deserts of Afghanistan, is another. This is a much poorer, less developed country. In 2011 the news from Pakistan, on Afghanistan's southern border, is less hopeful. There is a rising tide of extremism and political violence, and support for the Taliban. This has been inflamed by the war in Afghanistan and by the military attacks and killing of civilians by drone attacks in the border regions. Without peace and stability in Pakistan, can there ever be peace in Afghanistan?

A lasting peace

Among ordinary Afghans there is a powerful desire for a better future. The many brave people who are prepared to stand up to injustice, who engage in activism, teach, help the poor, challenge corruption and rebuild their towns and villages are the ones who in the end will win the support of the Afghan people.

When the foreign soldiers have returned safely to their families, when Afghan boys and girls can go to school and women can live without fear, there may be peace. It will need to be one that lasts, one that does not end only this chapter of history, but whole centuries of warfare.

The big questions

Since 2001 the Afghan conflict has been a painful period of history for Afghans and also for the Western powers. The view of what has been happening will vary greatly from one person to the next – a British or a Canadian soldier, an Afghan farmer or schoolgirl, a detainee in Bagram prison or Guantánamo Bay, a woman in Kabul, a Taliban fighter, an opium trader or a warlord, a human rights campaigner, a refugee, a Tajik, Pashtun or Hazara, an Afghan politician or a NATO general. Only by finding out the stories of all such people can we piece together the full picture of what has been happening and understand their experiences. Only by finding out about how governments work, about the work of the United Nations, about human rights and international law, can we begin to think about conflict resolution and the road to peace.

◀ *These Afghan schoolgirls at Balkh must be allowed to shape their own future.*

Viewpoints

"There is a long road ahead for Afghanistan, but with your help, I know that our people are capable of walking it, forging a path towards a future of peace, prosperity and equality."

Malalai Joya in *Raising My Voice*, 2009

"Places which were very safe last year are very unsafe now... If this conflict is not winnable, we need a political settlement."

Orzala Nemat, *Afghan Women's Network*, 2011

• Everyone hopes for a peaceful future, but just how that can be achieved involves difficult political decisions.

• Malalai Joya ends her book on an optimistic note, but do you think she would be prepared to accept compromise?

• Is Orzala Nemat more pessimistic, or just a realist? The truth may be that both idealism and compromise will be needed to resolve this conflict.

▶ *A carpet weaver in Bamiyan City.*

The big questions need discussion. What are the possible causes of terrorism? Why might individual humans or even governments commit such acts against others? Is it a reaction to injustice? An inability to bring about political change by any other methods? Religious extremism? Do terrorists ever achieve their political aims? What is the best way of countering terrorism? Within the law, or outside it? Can one fight injustice with injustice?

Are human rights universal? How can they be enforced? Is it acceptable for one country to go to war with another? If so, under what circumstances? Is there such a thing as a just war?

This Afghan war is not over yet, but we can already begin to think about its history – and learn its lessons.

Timeline

c1813-1907 The Great Game: rivalry between the Russian and British empires in Central Asia.

1839-42 The First Anglo-Afghan War.

1878-80 The Second Anglo-Afghan War.

1919 The Third Anglo-Afghan War.

1919 The British Empire recognizes Afghan independence.

1929-33 Power struggles and assassinations.

1933 Mohammed Zahir Shah becomes king.

1964 A democratic constitution is agreed upon.

1965 Founding of the Marxist People's Democratic Party of Afghanistan (PDPA).

1973 Zahir Shah is overthrown; Afghanistan becomes a republic.

1978 Communists of the PDPA seize power under Nur Muhammad Taraki.

1979 Power struggle and revolts occur. Taraki is murdered.

Soviet (Russian) invasion of Afghanistan. Resistance by the Western-backed Mujahideen lasts ten years.

1980 Babrak Kemal installed as leader by the Russians.

1986 Babrak Kemal replaced by Mohammad Najibullah.

1989 Russian withdrawal from Afghanistan.

1992 Najibullah overthrown. The Mujahideen capture Kabul. Civil war between factions and warlords.

1996 The Taliban faction captures Kabul. Fighting against the Northern Alliance.

2001 Al-Qaeda, a Saudi-led terrorist group based in Afghanistan, is accused of 9/11 terrorist attacks in the US. The Taliban government refuses to hand over al-Qaeda members.

US and British forces attack Afghanistan and support the Northern Alliance, who capture Kabul. Start of the current war in Afghanistan.

2002 Assembly appoints Hamid Karzai as president. International force, ISAF, is created and its operations begin to expand in Afghanistan.

2002 First detainees are taken to Guantánamo Bay.

2003-06 NATO takes command of international forces.

2004 Karzai wins presidential election.

2005 Parliamentary general election.

2009 Disputed presidential election; Karzai claims victory.

2010 Delayed general election. Foreign forces reach highest number, also most casualties.

2010 NATO agrees that Afghan forces will take over security in 2014.

2011 Osama bin Laden is shot dead in Pakistan by US Navy SEALS.

Glossary

atrocity A violent act of great cruelty or savagery.

bureaucracy Excessive government administration.

burqa A traditional form of women's robe in Afghanistan, covering the whole body and head, with only a mesh panel to see through.

cleric A priest or religious official.

civil war A war fought between two factions from the same nation.

coalition A political or military alliance.

communism A political movement intended to give power to the working class and state control of the economy.

conscript An ordinary citizen who is called up to fight for his or her country, as opposed to a professional soldier.

constitution The system of basic laws that set up a government and govern a country.

democracy A nation ruled by the people or by elected representatives of the people.

diplomat Someone who represents his or her nation when negotiating and making agreements with other nations.

electoral commission A body set up to ensure that an election is fair and valid.

embedding The placing of a journalist within a military force during a war.

established religion The official religion of a country.

ethnic group Any group of people who share the same descent, customs or language.

flogging Extreme whipping, as a punishment.

friendly fire During a battle, shooting at soldiers who are on the same side, generally by accident.

fundamentalism Believing in the literal truth of scripture (holy writing), or supporting the traditional forms of a religion.

guerrilla a) Warfare that consists of skirmishes, sabotage and running battles rather than pitched battles between large armies. b) A fighter engaged in such warfare.

insurgent Someone taking part in an armed rebellion or uprising.

international law The laws and treaties that govern the relations between nations.

irregular fighters Fighters belonging to an armed force that is not organized or structured in the usual way.

legal process The system of justice whereby a person is charged with an offense, allowed a legal defense and given a fair trial in court.

legislation The passing of laws.

militant A radical activist or fighter.

militia An armed force separate from a national army, made up of citizen volunteers or conscripts.

proxy Someone who carries out an action on behalf of someone else.

puritanical Following a strict and rigid moral or religious code, rejecting pleasure and amusement.

radicalize To become radical, adopting strong political views.

rendition Secretly sending detainees to foreign jails for interrogation, and possibly torture.

resistance A political and armed organization, often secret, operating against occupying forces or a repressive government.

secular Nonreligious.

Shari'a The religious law and practices of Islam, which have been interpreted in various ways by Muslim scholars. In some countries and regions, Shari'a forms the basis of civil law.

Shi'a A minority branch of the Islamic faith. Shi'a Muslims have different beliefs from the mainstream about the descendants of the prophet Muhammad and the role of the Islamic community.

sniper A marksman who targets individual enemy soldiers.

Sunni The mainstream branch of the Islamic faith, followed by a majority of the Afghan population.

task force A force set up to carry out a particular military operation.

vote rigging Cheating during an election, to make sure that one party wins.

For More Information

Books

Cornerstones of Freedom: The War in Afghanistan by Jennifer Zeiger (Children's Press, 2011)

Raising My Voice by Malalai Joya (Rider, 2009)

Welcome to My Country: Afghanistan by Deborah Fordyce (Franklin Watts, 2010)

Web sites

Due to the changing nature of Internet links, Rosen Publishing has developed an online list of Web sites related to the subject of this book. This site is updated regularly. Please use this link to access the list:

http://www.rosenlinks.com/OWD/Afghan

Index